# Baabra Cadabra

Maverick
Early Readers

**'Baabra Cadabra'**
An original concept by Jenny Moore


Illustrated by Indira Muzbulakova

**Published by MAVERICK ARTS PUBLISHING LTD**
Studio 11, City Business Centre, 6 Brighton Road,
Horsham, West Sussex, RH13 5BB

+44 (0)1403 256941

A CIP catalogue record for this book is available at the British Library.

**ISBN 978-1-84886-900-4**



Maverick publishing
www.maverickbooks.co.uk

Turquoise

This book is rated as: Turquoise Band (Guided Reading)

# Baabra Cadabra

By Jenny Moore

Illustrated by
Indira Muzbulakova

Shay the sheep loved magic.

She read books about magic.

She taught herself magic tricks.

She even dreamed about magic.

It was hard to do impressive tricks with such an old magic kit though. Shay's cards were worn and her wand was bent. Her top hat had a big hole in it.

She was saving up for the amazing

magic kit in the local shop window.

One day, there was a poster for a magic show in the shop window too. Shay ran home to tell Dad.

"There's a magic show tonight, with Gruffo the Great," she said. "Please, *please* can we go? I might learn some new tricks."

Dad grinned.

"Yes, we can go. Maybe Gruffo the Great can teach you a trick for turning a messy bedroom into a tidy one!"

The magic show was fantastic! There were no tidying-up tricks though.

Shay watched in wonder as Gruffo the Great pulled a huge bunch of flowers out of his hat. It was just like in her magic book.

She gasped out loud as Gruffo turned a tiny seed into a basket of carrots. She clapped her hooves at his amazing card tricks.

He made magic look easy.

“Now for a vanishing trick,” said Gruffo. “Who has a watch I can borrow?”

“Dad! Dad! Let him use yours. Please!” Shay begged.

Dad undid his watch and held it out for Gruffo. “You can borrow mine,” he said.

Gruffo covered Dad’s watch with a cloth and waved his wand.

“Baabra cadabra!” he cried. When he lifted the cloth, Dad’s watch was gone.

Everyone clapped and cheered... except for Dad.

“Where’s my watch?” he bleated.

“Don’t worry,” whispered Shay. “I know how this trick works. Your watch is safe in Gruffo’s pocket!”

Next, Gruffo made someone's bracelet vanish.

"Baabra cadabra!"

Then he made a gold pin disappear.

"Baabra cadabra!"

He made two phones vanish away at once!

"Baabra cadabra!"

"Now for *another* vanishing trick," said Gruffo. "I'll need some money for this one."

"I've got some money!" said Shay.

This was her chance to be part of the show.

Shay reached into her fleece pocket for her purse. She took out all the money she'd been saving for a new magic kit and handed it to Gruffo.

"Here it is!"

Gruffo the Great put a cloth over Shay's money and waved his magic wand.

"Baabra cadabra!"

He pulled the cloth away and Shay clapped her hooves. Her money had vanished.

Even though she knew how the trick worked, she was still impressed.

"And now for my final trick," said Gruffo, climbing into a big box in the middle of the stage. "I need you all to count up to twenty, then say the magic words."

Everyone counted to twenty and cried,

"Baabra cadabra!"

Nothing happened.

"Baabra cadabra!" they called again.

Still nothing happened.

“Perhaps we should open the box and check he’s alright,” said Dad.

He and Shay pulled up the lid, but the box was empty!

“Oh no,” said Dad, turning to the audience. “It looks like *Gruffo* has vanished this time, taking all our things with him. What about my watch, and the bracelet? What about the gold pin and the phones? What about Shay’s money? He’s tricked us all.”

The owner of the gold pin began to cry.

"That was a gift from my grandmother," she sobbed.

"Ring the police," cried the owner of the bracelet. "Tell them Gruffo the Great is a thief. He stole our things."

"We can't ring *anybody*," sniffed the owners of the missing phones.

"Wait," shouted Shay. "I think I know where Gruffo is."

"Where?" asked Dad.

"Right here," said Shay, pointing at the empty magic box. "I read about this trick in my magic book. I think there's a fake panel in the bottom of the box. Gruffo must be hiding under there, waiting for everyone to leave."

Dad examined the box. "Yes!" he said. "You're right."

Shay and Dad pulled up the fake panel with a "*Baabra cadabra!*"

There was Gruffo, clutching all their stolen things!

Everybody clapped and cheered.

"Well done, Shay," said Dad. "Making Gruffo reappear was the best trick of all!"

The police came and arrested Gruffo the Great.

"Good work finding the thief, Shay," said one of the officers. "You'd make a good detective."

Shay shook her head. "No," she said. "I'm going to be a magician when I grow up... a *good* magician though, not like Gruffo. I just need a bit more practise and a new magic kit."

Shay was at home the next day, working on her magic, when there was a knock at the door. It was the other animals whose things Gruffo had stolen.

"Hello Shay," they said, handing her a large parcel. "This is to say thank you for finding our things."

Shay unwrapped the parcel and grinned.

“Wow! The amazing magic kit from the shop window! Thank you!”

# Quiz

1. What was Shay saving up for?

a) A bike

b) A new set of cards

c) A magic kit

2. Whose magic show did Shay go to?

a) Gruffo the Great's

b) Griffo the Grand's

c) Gruffo the Greedy's

3. What does Gruffo steal from Shay's dad?

a) His glasses

b) His wallet

c) His watch

4. Where does Gruffo hide?

a) Beneath a fake panel in the box

b) Beneath a trap door

c) Behind the stage curtains

5. What does the police officer say to Shay?

a) "You'd make a good magician."

b) "You'd make a good detective."

c) "You'd make a good police officer."

*Turn over for answers* 

# Book Bands for Guided Reading

The Institute of Education book banding system is a scale of colours that reflects the various levels of reading difficulty. The bands are assigned by taking into account the content, the language style, the layout and phonics. Word, phrase and sentence level work is also taken into consideration.

Maverick Early Readers are a bright, attractive range of books covering the pink to white bands. All of these books have been book banded for guided reading to the industry standard and edited by a leading educational consultant.

To view the whole Maverick Readers scheme, visit our website at www.maverickearlyreaders.com

Or scan the QR code above to view our scheme instantly!

*Quiz Answers: 1c, 2a, 3c, 4a, 5b*